A LITTLE TASTE OF
SAN FRANCISCO

a little taste of
SAN FRANCISCO

Recipes for Classic Dishes

By Stephanie Rosenbaum Klassen

Illustrations by Courtney Jentzen

Bluestreak
BOOKS

Connected Dots Media would like to thank the team at Bluestreak Books for their generous work on this project, especially to publisher Chris Navratil for his smart, insightful creative inspiration.

Bluestreak Books is an imprint of Weldon Owen,
a Bonnier Publishing USA company
www.bonnierpublishingusa.com

Library of Congress-in-Publication Data is Available.

ISBN: 978-1-68188-349-6

First printed in 2018
10 9 8 7 6 5 4 3 2 1
2018 2019

Printed in China

Text and recipes by Stephanie Rosenbaum Klassen
Design by Margaux Keres
Illustrations by Courtney Jentzen

Produced exclusively for Bluestreak Books by Connected Dots Media,
www.connecteddotsmedia.com

CONTENTS

INTRODUCTION

San Francisco is a magical city, its spires and hills rising like a mirage out of the fog at the farthest edge of the Pacific frontier. It draws its citizens from all over the world. Walk through its neighborhoods, and you'll hear people speaking Spanish, Cantonese, Tagalog, Vietnamese, Farsi, Mandarin, Russian, and dozens more.

In this cosmopolitan city, a day might begin with piping-hot tea paired with *ha gow* and *shu mai*, bite-sized Chinese dumplings served in tiny storefronts on Clement Street. Or breakfast might be a thick slab of avocado toast and an almond-milk latte, downed at an Ocean Beach café next to surfers fueling up for some pre-work waves. Hip boutique bakeries line up their maple-bacon doughnuts and crunchy *kouign amanns* while the Mission's panaderias arrange their sugar-dusted Mexican sweet breads. The industrial-chic, third-wave coffeehouses meticulously measure the beans for their pour-over coffees.

San Francisco is an eater's paradise, crowded with restaurants whipping up everything from cheap eats to beyond-your-dreams innovative gastronomy. For cooks, the hardest part might be deciding what to make, thanks to a super-abundance of remarkable ingredients, from luscious Napa Valley olive oil to Dungeness crabs and wild salmon straight from the sea. Every week, farmers' markets full of farm-fresh produce turn our city streets into a glowing reminder of the Bay Area's natural bounty.

The stories in *A Little Taste of San Francisco* will whet your appetite for a trip to the City by the Bay or remind you to savor memorable experiences from previous visits. These recipes will bring the many flavors of San Francisco to your own kitchen. You'll learn how to make your own Chinese dumplings, Vietnamese sandwiches, and Mexican tacos. You'll find old-school classic main dishes like cioppino and Crab Louie; better-than-the-Wharf clam chowder in a bread bowl; North Beach tiramisù and drinks both spirited and sweet. Join us for a culinary journey up and down the hills of San Francisco, in the most delicious way.

1

DRINKS

A town built on the visions of sailors, dreamers, eccentrics, bohemians, artists, and everything in between: is it any surprise that this city, a cosmopolitan enclave perched at the last, wild edge of North America, enjoys a drink or two?

The Pisco Sour and its pineapple-sweet cousin, Pisco Punch, were born in the Bay Area. Irish Coffee, the perfect warm-up for fog-swept, chilly nights, made its stateside debut here; so did the Mai Tai, a tiki-bar classic reminiscent of balmier Pacific shores. These days, San Francisco is a mecca for modern mixologists, with bartenders taking their cues from top chefs to make their own seasonally inspired tinctures, syrups, bitters, and shrubs.

When we Bay Area denizens drink, we drink well, and probably we learn to take it a little for granted. Hard not to, with many of the country's best wine, craft beer, and spirits producers right in our backyard—along with fresh Meyer lemons ready to be squeezed into summer-afternoon lemonade, fruity *aguas frescas* ladled up in every taqueria, and the strongest coffee west of, well, the whole continental U.S. (even if Seattle might beg to differ). So, raise a glass and toast to life's good fortune.

3

MAI TAI

The Mai Tai was born in 1944 at Trader Vic's, the Bay Area's original tiki bar, whose ersatz exoticism spawned a craze for Polynesian-style drinks, food, and decor. These days, Bay Area rum connoisseurs and tiki-drink mavens slake their thirst at sophisticated hideaways like Smuggler's Cove, with its list of 500-plus rums that includes many rare and vintage bottles, or make a night of it at retro favorites like the Tonga Room in the Hotel Fairmont.

NOTE Orgeat, an almond syrup typically used for flavored coffee drinks and Italian sodas, is the Mai Tai's secret ingredient. Look for it among the coffee products in the grocery store.

SERVES 1

Cracked ice

2 ounces Jamaican dark rum

½ ounce orange curaçao

½ ounce fresh lime juice

Splash of Simple Syrup (page 5)

Splash of orgeat syrup

Ice cubes

½ ounce light rum, for a float (optional)

Paper parasol, lime slice, and/or orchid blossom for garnish

1 In a cocktail shaker filled with cracked ice, combine the dark rum, curaçao, lime juice, Simple Syrup, and orgeat. Shake well, then strain into a tall chilled goblet filled with ice cubes.

2 Float the light rum on top, if using. Garnish with the paper parasol, lime slice, and/or orchid blossom and serve right away.

PISCO SOUR

In the wake of the Gold Rush, everything and everyone arrived on the shores of the Barbary Coast. Thirsty sailors and tale-telling adventurers packed the wharfside saloons, and their favorite grog was a fiery Peruvian spirit known as pisco. Dressed up with lemon juice, sugar, and a frothy egg white, the Pisco Sour (along with its cousin, the pineapple-flavored Pisco Punch) soon became a favorite cocktail for San Franciscans like Jack London and Mark Twain.

SERVES 1

2 ounces pisco

¾ ounce Simple Syrup
(recipe follows)

¾ ounce fresh lemon juice, or
a combination of lemon and
lime juice

1 large egg white

Ice

A few drops of orange bitters

1 In a cocktail shaker, combine the pisco, Simple Syrup, lemon juice, and egg white. Shake briefly to emulsify. Add a handful of ice and shake vigorously until the drink is smooth and foamy.

2 Strain into a chilled cocktail glass. Garnish with a few drops of bitters and serve right away.

SIMPLE SYRUP

MAKES ABOUT ½ CUP

½ cup sugar

½ cup water

In a small saucepan over medium-high heat, combine the sugar and water and cook, stirring often, until the sugar has dissolved, about 5 minutes. Remove from the heat and let cool to room temperature. The syrup will keep in a tightly sealed jar in the refrigerator for up to 1 month.

IRISH COFFEE

Ding-ding-ding! goes the bell of the Hyde Street cable car, and shivering tourists scurry toward the glowing neon sign of the Buena Vista Café. Although this snug saloon at the corner of Hyde and Beach Streets has been serving locals and visitors alike since 1916, it was then-owner Jack Koeppler's introduction of Irish Coffee in 1952 that made its reputation. As legend has it, Koeppler first tasted the drink created by local chef Joe Sheridan when he and a group of American passengers were stranded by bad weather at Ireland's Shannon Airport. Laced with Irish whiskey, topped with thick, sweet cream, and served in a signature glass mug, this fortified coffee still makes an ideal fog chaser.

SERVES 1

¼ cup heavy cream

Hot water

¾ cup freshly made hot coffee

2 sugar cubes or
1 teaspoon sugar

1½ ounces Irish whiskey

1 In a small bowl or glass, whisk the cream until it thickens slightly but is still pourable.

2 Rinse a mug, preferably heatproof glass, with hot water and discard the water. Pour the hot coffee into the warmed mug. Add the sugar cubes and stir to dissolve. Add the whiskey and stir to mix.

3 Pour the thickened cream into the mug over the back of a spoon to float it on the top of the drink. Serve right away.

HORCHATA

This creamy, cinnamon-scented beverage is a popular favorite in San Francisco taquerias, where it's ladled out of big glass jars alongside brightly colored fruit-flavored *aguas frescas*. With a base made from rice, almonds, or melon seeds, it's a refreshing and dairy-free drink that pairs well with Carnitas Tacos (page 38).

SERVES 4

1¼ cups blanched almonds

1 cup raw white rice

One 3-inch piece cinnamon stick

2½ cups hot water

½ cup sugar or agave syrup, or to taste

2 cups cold water or rice milk

Ground cinnamon for dusting

1 In a large heatproof bowl, combine the almonds, rice, cinnamon stick, and hot water and stir to mix. Let cool, then cover and refrigerate for at least 8 hours or up to overnight.

2 Pour the almond mixture into a blender. Add the sugar and blend on high speed until smooth, 2 to 3 minutes. Pour through a fine-mesh sieve into a bowl, pressing on the solids in the sieve to extract any remaining liquid.

3 Pour the *horchata* into a large pitcher and add the cold water. Refrigerate until well chilled, at least 1 hour and up to 24 hours.

4 Serve in tall glasses over ice, dusted with cinnamon.

BACKYARD MEYER LEMONADE

Stroll through one of the city's sunnier southern neighborhoods, peer over a backyard fence, and you're likely to spy a fragrant Meyer lemon tree laden with brilliant yellow fruit. Juicier, sweeter, and more aromatic than a regular lemon, Meyers are used by San Franciscans in everything from cocktails to salad dressing to desserts. They're most prolific in the wintertime, cheering up chilly days with their sunshiny glow.

SERVES 4

4 to 6 Meyer lemons

½ cup sugar, honey, or agave syrup

3 cups water, or to taste

Ice

Fresh mint or lemon verbena sprigs for garnish

1 Using a vegetable peeler, remove the zest from 2 of the lemons in long strips. In a saucepan over medium-low heat, combine the zest strips, sugar, and ½ cup water. Bring to a gentle simmer and cook, stirring, until the sugar is dissolved, about 5 minutes. Remove the syrup from the heat and let cool to room temperature.

2 Juice the 2 zested lemons plus more as needed to get about 1 cup juice. Strain the lemon-infused syrup into a large pitcher. Add the lemon juice and the remaining 2½ cups water and stir to mix. Add more water to taste, if needed. Refrigerate until well chilled, at least 1 hour and up to 24 hours.

3 Pour the lemonade into tall glasses over ice. Garnish with the mint sprigs and serve right away.

AGUAS FRESCAS

These bright, tangy, not-too-sweet drinks are served at every taqueria and neighborhood Mexican restaurant. Fresh fruit is puréed with plenty of water and lightly sweetened, sometimes with a splash of fresh citrus. Depending on what's in season, look for *sandía* (watermelon), *fresa* (strawberry), Jamaica (made from the tart, magenta-colored blossoms of the hibiscus bush), *tamarindo* (tamarind), or *piña* (pineapple). Experiment with your own combinations; if necessary, strain out seeds or excess pulp after puréeing.

NOTE: Look for dried hibiscus blossoms, often labeled as Jamaica, in stores specializing in Mexican and Latin American products.

EACH RECIPE SERVES 4

WATERMELON (SANDIA)

6 cups seedless watermelon chunks

¼ cup sugar, or to taste

2 tablespoons fresh lime juice

¼ teaspoon kosher salt

2 cups water

Ice

Lime wedges for garnish (optional)

1 In a blender, combine the watermelon, sugar, lime juice, salt, and water, working in batches if necessary, and blend at high speed until smooth, 30 to 60 seconds.

2 Pour the watermelon mixture through a fine-mesh sieve into a large pitcher. Discard the solids. Refrigerate until well chilled, at least 1 hour and up to 24 hours.

3 Pour into tall glasses over ice. Garnish with lime wedges, if using, and serve right away.

MANGO

2 cups chopped ripe mango
(2 large mangoes)

⅓ cup sugar, or to taste

3 tablespoons fresh lime or
lemon juice

4 cups water

Ice

Lime or lemon wedges
for garnish

1 In a blender, combine the mango, sugar, lime or lemon juice, and 1 cup of
the water. Blend at high speed until smooth, 30 to 60 seconds.

2 Pour the mango mixture into a large pitcher, add the remaining 3 cups
water, and stir to mix well. If the drink seems too thick, add more water to
taste. Refrigerate until well chilled, at least 1 hour and up to 24 hours.

3 Pour into tall glasses over ice. Garnish with lime or lemon wedges and
serve right away.

HIBISCUS (JAMAICA)

1 cup dried hibiscus flowers
(see Note)

⅓ cup sugar

8 cups water

2 tablespoons fresh lemon
or lime juice

Ice

1 In a large pot, combine the hibiscus flowers, sugar, and water and bring to
a boil over high heat, stirring to dissolve the sugar. Reduce the heat to low
and simmer until well flavored and colored, about 10 minutes. Remove from
the heat and let cool.

2 Pour the hibiscus mixture through a fine-mesh sieve into a large pitcher.
Discard the solids. Refrigerate until well chilled, at least 3 hours and up to
24 hours. Add the lemon juice and stir well.

3 Pour into tall glasses over ice and serve right away.

APPETIZERS & SMALL BITES

San Francisco is a city built for noshers and grazers. From elegant restaurants to Formica-table storefronts, Chinese dim sum dumplings and barbecued pork buns beckon from loaded carts and steamers. Little toasts known as bruschetta make a perfect starter with a glass of Prosecco on a warm evening. What would a home-team baseball game be without a fat cone of pungent garlic fries between innings? Artichokes grow near here; so do some of the country's best oysters, which locals love to toss on the grill to add a little smoky allure.

The Bay Area's explosion of artisanally made everything, from bread, jam, and chocolate to cheese, charcuterie, and pickles has been a delicious boon to the city's food lovers. Small-batch farmstead cheeses, made from the milk of local cows, sheep, and goats, are prized; so are the many bakeries making fantastic sweet and savory pastries and breads. Street foods from all around the world have found a home here, in food trucks and storefronts, pop-up restaurants and farmers' markets. All you need is an open mind and an eager belly. Let's eat!

Thank you Enjoy

BRUSCHETTA

The Bay Area's mild, marine-moderated climate offers perfect conditions for many Mediterranean plants. Breathe deep, and you'll catch the scent of rosemary, thyme, and lavender; spy into a well-cultivated backyard, and you might find a tangle of fava bean plants in spring or a shady fig tree dangling plump black figs in early summer and again in the early autumn.

Both fava beans and figs make wonderful toppings for crisp *bruschetta* of toasted baguette, perfect with a glass of sparkling wine from Mendocino's Anderson Valley.

EACH RECIPE SERVES 4

FAVA BEAN

½ baguette, thinly sliced

1 clove garlic, halved

3 tablespoons extra-virgin olive oil

2 pounds fava beans

Salt and freshly ground black pepper

Juice of ½ lemon

Pecorino romano cheese shavings for garnish

Small handful of fresh mint leaves, thinly sliced, for garnish

1 Preheat the oven to 350°F. Arrange the baguette slices on a baking sheet. Lightly toast in the oven until just crisp, about 5 minutes. Remove from the oven and rub the top of each piece with the cut side of a garlic clove. Brush the tops with 2 tablespoons of the olive oil. Set aside.

2 Fill a medium saucepan about halfway with water and bring to a boil over high heat. Meanwhile, shell the fava beans. Add the fava beans to the boiling water and blanch for about 2 minutes. Drain in a colander set in the sink and rinse under cold running water to stop the cooking. Drain again thoroughly and set aside to cool. When the beans are cool enough to handle,

pinch off the tough outer skin. Discard the skins and set the tender green fava beans aside.

3 In a small saucepan over low heat, combine the favas with a few tablespoons of water, the remaining 1 tablespoon olive oil, and a pinch of salt. Cook, stirring often, until the favas are tender, about 5 minutes. Remove from the heat, add the lemon juice, and stir to mix well.

4 Using a fork or potato masher, mash the fava mixture into a rough paste. Season with salt and freshly ground pepper to taste.

5 Spread a generous spoonful of the fava mixture on each baguette slice. Top each with a cheese shaving or two and a few pieces of mint. Serve right away.

FIG, RICOTTA, AND WALNUT

½ baguette, cut into 16 thin slices

2 tablespoons extra-virgin olive oil

¾ cup ricotta cheese

½ cup walnut halves or pieces, lightly toasted and coarsely chopped

8 ripe figs, halved

Fresh thyme leaves for garnish

1 Preheat the oven to 350°F. Arrange the baguette slices on a baking sheet. Lightly toast in the oven until just crisp, about 5 minutes. Remove from the oven and brush the tops with the olive oil. Leave the oven on.

2 Spread a scant teaspoonful of the ricotta on each baguette slice. Sprinkle with the walnuts and top each with a fig half, cut side up. Return to the oven and bake just until the ricotta is heated through and the figs soften, about 3 minutes.

3 Sprinkle each *bruschetta* with a few thyme leaves and serve right away.

SHRIMP DUMPLINGS

A dim sum lunch isn't complete without a steamer basket (or two) of sweet shrimp wrapped in plump, translucent blankets of dough. Called *ha gow* in Cantonese, these popular dumplings are actually fairly easy to make start to finish from scratch. Wheat starch, available in Asian grocery stores or online, is the key ingredient in homemade dough for authentic wrappers.

If you don't want to make your own dough, you can use premade 3-inch dumpling or gyoza (pot sticker) wrappers, also available at Asian groceries.

MAKES 24 DUMPLINGS; SERVES 4 TO 6

FOR THE DOUGH:

1 cup wheat starch
(see recipe introduction)

½ cup tapioca starch

⅛ teaspoon kosher salt

1 cup minus 2 tablespoons
boiling water

1 tablespoon vegetable oil

FOR THE FILLING:

¾ pound shrimp, peeled,
deveined, and roughly chopped

1 scallion, white and tender
green part only, minced

1½ tablespoons Chinese rice
wine

1½ teaspoons fresh grated
ginger

¾ teaspoon kosher salt

Generous pinch of ground
white pepper

1 To make the dough, in a heatproof bowl, whisk together the wheat starch, tapioca starch, and salt. Add the boiling water and oil and stir well to form a thick dough. Turn the dough out onto a clean work surface and knead until smooth (the texture should feel like modeling clay), about 2 minutes. Wrap loosely in plastic wrap and let the dough come to room temperature, about 10 minutes.

2 Divide the dough into 4 equal pieces. Roll each piece between your palms into a rope about 8 inches long, then place the ropes on a clean work surface and cut each into 6 equal pieces. Roll each dough piece into a ball and then, using a rolling pin, roll each into a round about 3 inches in diameter.

3 To make the filling, in a bowl, combine the shrimp, scallion, rice wine, ginger, salt and pepper. Stir gently to mix well.

4 Place a rounded teaspoon of filling in the center of a dough round or wrapper. Fold the wrapper over the filling to make a half-moon shape and pinch or crimp with the tines of a fork to seal. Set aside. Repeat with the remaining wrappers and filling.

5 Place a rack in a pot large enough to hold a bamboo steamer. Add water to come up just below the bottom of steamer. Bring the water to a boil over high heat.

6 Line a bamboo steamer with parchment paper. Place 4 to 6 dumplings in the steamer, spacing them so they don't touch. Cover the steamer and lower it onto the rack.

7 Cover the pot and steam the dumplings until wrappers are translucent and shrimp filling is pink, 5 to 6 minutes. Remove the steamer from the pot, let the dumplings cool slightly, and serve. Repeat with the remaining dumplings.

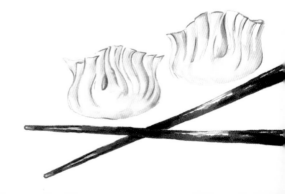

BALLPARK GARLIC FRIES

Forget peanuts and Cracker Jack—as any Giants fan can tell you, Gilroy Garlic Fries are *the* snack to have at a Giants baseball game. Salty, moreish, and pungent with garlic, these fries are surprisingly simple to reproduce at home. The name comes from the farming town of Gilroy, where the majority of California's garlic is grown.

SERVES 4 TO 6

4 cups vegetable oil

1 pound frozen French fries

⅓ cup extra-virgin olive oil

2 tablespoons minced fresh garlic

2 tablespoons minced fresh flat-leaf parsley

Kosher salt and freshly ground black pepper

1 In a deep fryer, Dutch oven, or heavy-bottomed saucepan over medium-high heat, heat the vegetable oil to 375°F on a deep-frying thermometer.

2 Using a skimmer or slotted spoon and working in batches if necessary to avoid crowding, add the fries to the hot oil and cook, turning once, until deep golden brown, about 15 minutes total.

3 Meanwhile, in a small bowl, whisk together the olive oil and garlic.

4 Using the skimmer, transfer the fries to a plate lined with paper towels to drain. Transfer the drained fries to a large bowl. Pour the olive oil mixture over the fries, tossing to coat evenly. Add the parsley and season to taste with salt and pepper. Toss again and serve right away.

GRILLED ARTICHOKES WITH HERB BUTTER

Some of the best artichokes in the country are grown in the fog-kissed fields of California's Central Coast, south of San Francisco between Half Moon Bay and Monterey. For lovers of this delicious thistle, a road trip down the coast should always include a stop in Pescadero for a hot loaf of artichoke bread at Arcangeli's or a bowl of cream of artichoke soup at the historic Duarte's Tavern. At home, it's easy to give fresh artichokes a smoky finish on the grill.

SERVES 4

Kosher salt

4 large globe artichokes

Olive oil for brushing

2 lemons, halved

2 tablespoons finely chopped fresh herbs such as tarragon, basil, or flat-leaf parsley, or a combination

½ cup unsalted butter, melted

1 Bring a large pot of lightly salted water to a boil over high heat. Using a serrated knife, trim off about 1 inch of the top of each artichoke, cut the stem ends off flush with the bottom, and cut each in half lengthwise.

2 Add the artichokes to the boiling water and cook until a small knife inserted into the thickest part of the base of one slides through the flesh easily, about 20 minutes. Meanwhile, build a hot fire in a charcoal grill and generously oil the grill rack.

3 Drain thoroughly and pat dry. Brush the halves on all sides lightly with olive oil and sprinkle them all over with the juice of 1 lemon. Season with salt.

4 Arrange the artichokes cut-side down on the grill rack over direct heat and grill until nicely browned on both sides, about 10 minutes total.

5 In a bowl, combine the herbs, juice of the remaining lemon, and melted butter. Serve with artichokes for dipping.

BARBECUED OYSTERS

About 50 miles north of San Francisco, the estuaries of Tomales Bay—balanced between salt and fresh water by daily tidal flows—support a rich ecosystem of marine and wetlands species, including superlative shellfish. For a delicious change of pace, try a local delicacy: oysters thrown on the grill, painted with barbecue sauce, and slurped down hot and succulent in their own salty Pacific juices.

 SERVES 4

1 dozen large oysters, scrubbed

1 cup of your favorite barbecue sauce

1 Build a medium-hot fire in a charcoal or wood grill or preheat a gas grill to medium-high. Place the oysters, bottom-side down, on the grill. Cover and cook until the shells begin to crack open, about 2 minutes. (Discard any oysters that do not open.)

2 Transfer the oysters to a baking sheet and let cool for a few minutes. Using an oyster knife, loosen the top shell and remove. Gently wiggle the knife under each oyster to loosen it from the shell. Brush a small amount of the barbecue sauce over each oyster. Return the oysters to the grill, shell-side down, and cook for another minute to heat through. Transfer the oysters to a platter and serve right away.

VARIATIONS

Instead of barbecue sauce, try these flavored butters:

LIME-SRIRACHA Combine the juice of 2 limes with ½ cup melted unsalted butter. Add Sriracha sauce to taste.

MISO-GINGER Combine 1 tablespoon miso paste and 1 teaspoon peeled and grated fresh ginger with ½ cup melted unsalted butter.

CALIFORNIA SNACKING PLATE

This salty, savory, mix-and-match platter of cheeses, charcuterie, and condiments might start off as a snack, but with so many remarkable artisan food producers in the Bay Area, it's easy to lay out an abundant platter that can double as dinner. It's a delectable way to highlight the many high-quality cheesemakers, picklers, charcuterie producers, and condiment makers in San Francisco and beyond. It's a perfect choice for a holiday open house, a relaxed cocktail party, or a fun get-together at any time.

This recipe includes one idea for dressing up your favorite olives with an overnight soak in a bath of olive oil flavored with fresh herbs, garlic, and citrus peel. Use it as an inspiration for other combos of your own.

SERVES 2–4

1 loaf sourdough bread or 1 baguette, thinly sliced

1 fresh or lightly aged goat cheese, such as Cypress Grove's Humboldt Fog or Purple Haze

1 wedge of firm aged cow's milk cheese, such as Vella Dry Jack or Valley Ford Estero Gold

1 wedge of blue cheese, such as Point Reyes Original Blue

1 wedge of triple-crème cheese, such as Cowgirl Creamery Mt Tam or Red Hawk

A selection of charcuterie, such as salami, prosciutto, or 'nduja

Pickled vegetables

Chutney, fig jam, quince paste (membrillo) or citrus marmalade

Marinated Olives with Herbs, Garlic, and Citrus (recipe follows)

1 Arrange the bread, cheeses, charcuterie, pickled onions, jams, and olives on a large serving platter or board and serve.

MARINATED OLIVES WITH HERBS, GARLIC, AND CITRUS

MAKES ABOUT 1½ CUPS

¾ cup Picholine or other flavorful green olives

¾ cup Niçoise or Kalamata olives

⅓ cup extra-virgin olive oil

1 clove garlic, finely minced

1 teaspoon minced fresh thyme or rosemary

3 long strips orange or lemon zest

In a bowl, combine the olives, olive oil, garlic, thyme, and orange zest and stir to mix well.

Cover the olive mixture and let marinate at room temperature for at least 24 hours and up to 2 days, stirring occasionally. Serve at room temperature.

Transfer any remaining marinated olives to a jar, cover tightly, and store in the refrigerator for up to 1 month.

SALADS, SANDWICHES & SOUP

Kale salads, beet salads, warm goat-cheese salads, and more fill the menus of San Francisco's many restaurants; this city takes its greens seriously. A beautiful array of farmers' market greens—mesclun mixes, crisp heads of Little Gem lettuce, delicate rosettes of mâche, succulent purslane, tangy miner's lettuce, and wispy microgreens—thrives in abundance on farms in and around this great city. They're tossed in expressive mixes by innovative chefs seeking ways to showcase the area's best produce.

Sandwiches, too, rise above the usual lunchtime traditions, built with great bread and locally raised and cured meats and local cheeses, layered with plenty of pickled vegetables, fresh herbs, and inventive condiments. And the soups follow suit, composed with fresh ingredients from local waters and farms; this chapter includes a favorite San Francisco classic, Clam Chowder in a Sourdough Bread Bowl— a perfect rich and creamy seafood combo.

25

FARMERS' MARKET GREENS WITH BAKED GOAT CHEESE TOASTS

This simple French-inspired salad, introduced and popularized stateside by Alice Waters at Chez Panisse, is a hallmark of California cuisine and introduced many to the soft, mild goat cheese known as chèvre. Look for a mix of soft, sturdy, sweet, and pungent greens at the farmers' market for the mix; each season will inspire different ideas.

SERVES 4

One 4-ounce log chèvre or other fresh goat's-milk cheese, sliced into 8 rounds

¾ cup extra-virgin olive oil

Leaves from 4 sprigs fresh thyme

1 small shallot, finely minced

3 tablespoons red wine vinegar

Kosher salt and freshly ground black pepper

8 slices baguette

1 tablespoon melted butter or olive oil

2 cloves garlic, halved

1 cup dried bread crumbs

1 teaspoon dried thyme

6 cups mixed lettuces

1 Put the goat cheese rounds in a medium bowl. Drizzle with ¼ cup of the olive oil and sprinkle with the fresh thyme leaves. Turn gently to coat. Let marinate in the refrigerator for at least 12 hours and up to 24 hours.

2 In a small bowl, combine the shallot and vinegar and let stand at room temperature for about 20 minutes. Whisk in the remaining ½ cup olive oil and salt and pepper to taste. Set aside. Preheat the oven to 350°F.

3 Arrange the baguette slices on a baking sheet and brush both sides
with the melted butter. Bake, turning once, until lightly toasted, 5 to
7 minutes total. Rub the top sides of the toasted bread with the cut sides of
the garlic cloves and set aside.

4 Raise the oven temperature to 400°F. In a bowl, toss together the bread
crumbs and dried thyme. Remove the goat cheese from the marinade and
roll the rounds in the bread-crumb mixture until evenly coated. Arrange the
coated rounds on a clean baking sheet and bake until hot and beginning to
brown, about 6 minutes.

5 Toss the lettuce with the vinegar-shallot mixture. Divide the dressed
lettuces among 4 plates. Arrange 2 baguette slices and 2 rounds of goat
cheese on each plate and serve right away.

CRAB LOUIE

For over 100 years, Swan's Oyster Depot in Nob Hill has served up pristine fresh seafood. Behind the bar, the expert staff—many who have worked there for decades—are in constant motion, arranging shrimp cocktails, shucking oysters and clams, and, of course, assembling the hundreds of plates of Crab Louie that slide across the white marble counter every day.

Crab Louie dates back to the early part of the twentieth century, when it was a staple in San Francisco's grand hotels. What makes Swan's version stand out are the big, sweet chunks of fresh lump crabmeat they use. If you can't get whole crabs, look for good quality lump crabmeat from your local fishmonger. Some recipes add a splash of lemon juice, a dash of Worcestershire sauce, or a dab of prepared horseradish to the dressing; feel free to adjust the flavors to your own taste.

SERVES 4 TO 6

FOR THE DRESSING:

1 cup mayonnaise

¼ cup ketchup

¼ cup sweet pickle relish

¼ cup finely chopped scallions

1 hard-boiled egg, peeled and finely chopped

2 tablespoons chopped black olives

¼ teaspoon paprika

FOR THE SALAD:

1 large head iceberg or romaine lettuce

Fresh lump crabmeat from 2 large Dungeness crabs, about 2 pounds each (about 4 cups meat total)

2 tomatoes, cut into wedges

Lemon wedges for serving

1 To make the dressing, in a bowl, stir together the mayonnaise, ketchup, relish, scallions, egg, olives, and paprika until well mixed.

2 To assemble the salad, core the lettuce and shred finely. In a bowl, toss the lettuce with about ½ cup of the dressing. Divide the dressed lettuce among chilled plates. Top with the crabmeat, dividing it evenly. Spoon a little more of the dressing over the crab. Add the tomato and lemon wedges to each plate. Serve right away, with the remaining dressing on the side.

CLAM CHOWDER IN A SOURDOUGH BREAD BOWL

Clam chowder in a sourdough bread bowl is offered by nearly every seafood counter clustered along Fisherman's Wharf. Although sourdough bread has a long history in California, chowder in a bread bowl didn't become a popular tourist item until the local Boudin Bakery chain started offering it at its cafés along the wharf in the late 1980s. Here is a lighter, creamier version to showcase sweet, delicate Manila clams.

SERVES 4 TO 6

4 pounds small Manila clams

1 tablespoon unsalted butter

4 strips bacon, chopped

2 sprigs fresh thyme

1 celery rib, diced

1 leek, white part only, thinly sliced and thoroughly rinsed and dried

4 Yukon Gold potatoes, peeled and cut into bite-sized cubes

½ cup dry white wine

1 bay leaf

4 to 6 small sourdough boules (round loaves)

1 cup whole milk

1 cup heavy cream

Paprika and chopped fresh flat-leaf parsley for garnish

1 Rinse the clams thoroughly under cold running water, discarding any clams with broken or open shells. Put the clams in a large, heavy saucepan, cover with 4 cups water, and place over medium-high heat. Cover, bring to a boil, and cook until the clams have opened, 5 to 7 minutes. Discard any clams that do not open.

2 Using a slotted spoon, transfer the clams to a bowl and set aside to cool. Strain the cooking liquid remaining in the pot into a bowl through a fine-mesh sieve. Discard any sand or sediment in the sieve and reserve the strained liquid. When the clams are cool enough to handle, remove from the shells and set aside.

3 In a soup pot or large saucepan over medium-low heat, melt the butter. Add the bacon and thyme and cook, stirring, until the bacon has rendered its fat but hasn't browned, about 4 minutes. Add the celery, leek, and potatoes and cook, stirring, until the leek is soft, 6 to 8 minutes. Add the wine and cook until nearly evaporated. Add the reserved clam liquid and bay leaf. Cover the pot partially and cook until the potatoes are tender, 10 to 15 minutes.

4 Meanwhile, preheat the oven to 325°F. Slice the tops off the boules. Remove enough bread from inside of each to form a bowl. Place the hollowed-out boules on a baking sheet and bake for 5 minutes, until the crusts have crisped and the boules are warm.

5 Add the milk, cream, and cooked clams to the soup. Cook until the soup comes to a gentle simmer (do not let boil). Season to taste with salt and pepper.

6 To serve, ladle the soup into the boules, sprinkle lightly with paprika and parsley, and serve hot.

TOFU BÁNH MÌ

Vietnamese sandwiches are a San Francisco staple, arriving with the first post-war wave of Vietnamese immigration in the 1970s and becoming a part of the city's culinary landscape. The sandwiches blend French-colonist influence (French bread, a taste for charcuterie and pâté) with the Vietnamese fondness for pickles, fresh herbs, and spicy heat.

For best results, make the pickled daikon and carrots at least 1 day before serving.

SERVES 4

FOR THE PICKLES:

1 large daikon, peeled and cut into matchsticks

1 large carrot, peeled and cut into matchsticks

1 teaspoon sugar, plus ¼ cup

½ teaspoon kosher salt

FOR THE SANDWICH:

¾ cup distilled white vinegar

½ cup water

4 French baguette–style rolls

4 tablespoons mayonnaise, preferably Kewpie

Soy sauce or Maggi seasoning sauce for drizzling

Two 6-ounce packages baked tofu, thinly sliced

1 cucumber, peeled and thinly sliced

12 sprigs fresh cilantro or Thai basil

2 jalapeño chiles, thinly sliced (remove some or all of the seeds if you like less heat)

1 To make the pickles, in a large bowl, combine the daikon, carrot, 1 teaspoon sugar, and salt. Using your fingers, massage the salt and sugar into the daikon and carrot sticks. When the vegetables feel pliable and soft, after about 10 minutes, rinse under cold running water. Drain well and pack into a clean glass 1-quart jar.

2 In a bowl, combine the vinegar, water, and ¼ cup sugar and stir to
dissolve the sugar. Pour the vinegar mixture into the jar over the
vegetables. Cover and refrigerate for at least 8 hours or up to 1 week.
Once pickled, the vegetables may have a pungent odor, but the flavor
will be mild. Preheat the oven to 325°F.

3 To assemble the sandwiches, split the rolls in half lengthwise about
three-fourths of the way through, so that the two halves open but are still
attached at the seam, like a book. Hollow out the cut sides of the rolls with
a spoon.

4 Arrange the rolls on a baking sheet and place in the oven until warmed
through and lightly toasted, about 5 minutes.

5 Spread the inside of each warm roll with 1 tablespoon mayonnaise.
Drizzle with soy sauce. Divide the tofu slices between the cavities. Layer
on the cucumber slices, cilantro sprigs, and jalapeño slices and top with
the daikon and carrot pickles. Close the halves, pressing down gently to help
the ingredients hold together, and serve right away.

AVOCADO TOAST

The snack that launched a million Instagram posts. Californians have been topping their bread with slices of ripe avocado since at least the mid 1900s, when recipes started showing up in California cookbooks and newspapers.

In San Francisco, aficionados enjoy avocado toast in combinations ranging from the pure and simple to the gorgeously baroque. But while there is no shortage of discerning cafés dishing out $10 versions, many of us love it best at home, where we can use avocados when they reach the perfect moment of ripeness. The only requirement besides that luscious California avocado and our favorite add-ons is a fabulous nutty, crusty, rustic bread.

SERVES 2

2 to 4 slices fresh crusty bread, preferably whole-grain

2 ripe avocados, pitted and peeled

Extra-virgin olive oil

Flaky sea salt

Red pepper flakes or coarsely ground black pepper

1 Toast the bread. Slice the avocados or mash roughly in a bowl with a fork.

2 Arrange the avocado on the toast. Drizzle with olive oil, sprinkle with sea salt and red pepper flakes, and serve right away.

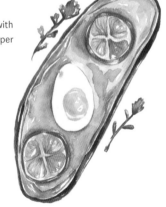

VARIATIONS

Every Californian has his or her own special variation of avocado toast. Some start with a dense, grainy German-style bread; others like a light, crusty ciabatta or sourdough slice. Instead of red pepper flakes, try flavorful chile powders like piment d'Esplette, Marash, or Aleppo.

Here are a few other favorite toppings:

Poached egg

Sliced hard-boiled egg

Crumbled feta cheese and small or chopped fresh mint leaves

Thinly sliced radishes and cucumbers

Sungold or Sweet 100 cherry tomatoes, halved

Sardines and minced preserved lemon

Uni (fresh sea urchin)

Dukkah (Egyptian nut-seed-spice seasoning mix)

Za'atar (Middle Eastern thyme-sesame-sumac seasoning mix)

Gomasio (Japanese sesame salt)

Sauerkraut

Pickled red onion

Seedy mix: dry-toasted sunflower, pumpkin, sesame, flax, cumin, and fennel seeds

Everything-bagel mix: dried onion flakes, poppy seeds, sesame seeds, and kosher salt

MAIN DISHES

San Francisco has more restaurants per person than any city in the United States—roughly one restaurant for every 100 people, although that's without counting the food trucks, street-fair stalls, and pop-up eateries. People might say they're coming to San Francisco to stroll the Golden Gate Bridge, explore Alcatraz, ride a cable car or snap a selfie in Haight-Ashbury, but year after year, surveys reveal that they *really* come here for the food.

Poised at the edge of the country, facing the Pacific Rim with America at its back, San Francisco has always had a global outlook. Sure, you'll find all-American burgers and classic steakhouses here, but locals know that you can eat your way around the world without ever leaving the city. A diverse and gastronomically curious population has made San Francisco a truly welcoming place for cooks and restaurateurs of all nations—and one of the most exciting destinations for adventurous eaters.

It's almost impossible to pick one quintessential San Francisco dish. Some folks would vote for the Mission-style burrito, inspired by Mexico but born in California; others for local seafood classics like cioppino and Dungeness crab. Whether you're sitting down for a 10-course tasting menu or grabbing a taco to-go, there's no better place to eat than the City by the Bay.

CARNITAS TACOS

Just about every San Franciscan can name their favorite taqueria. And while carne asada (grilled steak) may satisfy, and lengua (tongue) may delight, carnitas reigns supreme. Flavorful chunks of pork shoulder or country-style boneless ribs are marinated overnight with seasonings and citrus juices, then braised confit-style in lard. Just before serving, the fork-tender meat is crisped up in a hot pan, then wrapped in warm tortillas and topped with onion and cilantro. Look for fresh lard in a good-quality butcher shop.

SERVES 4 TO 6

2½ pounds boneless pork shoulder or country-style ribs, cut into 3-inch cubes

1 yellow onion, thinly sliced

4 cloves garlic, crushed

3 tablespoons fresh orange juice

1 tablespoon fresh lime juice

1 tablespoon kosher salt

2 teaspoons dried Mexican oregano

⅓ cup lard or vegetable oil, plus 1 tablespoon

12 corn tortillas, warmed

Lime wedges, chopped white onion, fresh cilantro sprigs, and your favorite salsa for serving

1 In a large bowl, toss the pork cubes with the onion, garlic, orange and lime juices, salt, oregano. Cover and refrigerate for 8 to 12 hours.

2 Preheat the oven to 275°F. Melt the ⅓ cup lard in a large Dutch oven or other heavy-bottomed ovenproof pot with a lid. Add the pork with its marinade. Bring to a simmer. Cover the pot and transfer to the oven. Cook, stirring occasionally, until the pork is fork-tender, 2 to 2½ hours.

3 Drain off the liquid. Let the pork cool slightly, then shred into bite-sized pieces, discarding any large pieces of fat. In a large skillet, heat the 1 tablespoon lard until hot. Add the pork and cook, stirring frequently, until crisped and browned on the edges, about 5 minutes. Serve right away, accompanied by the warmed corn tortillas, lime wedges, chopped white onion, cilantro sprigs, and salsa.

CHILLED DUNGENESS CRAB WITH MEYER LEMON–HERB VINAIGRETTE

The opening of the winter Dungeness crab season is front-page news (and big business) on the California coast. Fresh crab for Thanksgiving, Christmas, and New Year's Eve is a long-standing tradition in the Bay Area. During their peak season, they can be found freshly cooked, cleaned, and cracked in supermarkets and grocery stores across the city as well as at Fisherman's Wharf. Don't forget to pick up a loaf of sourdough bread and a lively California Chardonnay (or craft-beer IPA) to go with your crab. If you don't want to marinate the crab, serve the lemon vinaigrette on the side as a dipping sauce.

SERVES 4 TO 6

½ cup extra-virgin olive oil

¼ cup fresh Meyer lemon juice

2 tablespoons chopped fresh herbs such as dill, parsley, or tarragon, or a combination

1 small bunch fresh chives, finely chopped (about ¼ cup)

1 clove garlic, minced

Kosher salt and freshly ground black pepper

3 Dungeness crabs, about 1½ pounds each, cooked, cleaned, and cracked

1 In a large bowl, whisk together the olive oil, lemon juice, herbs, chives, and garlic. Season with salt and pepper to taste.

2 Add the crab pieces to the marinade and stir well to coat. Cover and place in the refrigerator to marinate for 2 to 3 hours.

3 Pile the crab pieces on a platter. Provide a nutcracker and crab fork for each diner, as well as a bowl for shells, and serve right away.

PETRALE SOLE DORÉ

Petrale (pronounced "pet-TRA-lee") sole, a flounder native to the Pacific, has delicate, mild-flavored fillets that make it a favorite of home cooks and chefs alike. It's sold in local fish markets and is a best-selling item on many local menus. This classic cooking method—called *doré*, or golden, for the burnished color of the pan-fried egg coating—also works well for Pacific sand dabs.

SERVES 2

2 petrale sole fillets, about 6 ounces each

Kosher salt and freshly ground black pepper

¼ cup all-purpose flour

2 large eggs

2 teaspoons unsalted butter, plus 3 tablespoons

2 teaspoons olive oil

2 tablespoons capers, drained and coarsely chopped

1 tablespoon chopped fresh flat-leaf parsley

1 tablespoon fresh Meyer lemon juice

1 Meyer lemon, cut into wedges, for serving

1 Season the fish on both sides with salt and pepper and set aside. Spread the flour on a plate or piece of waxed paper. Put eggs in a large, shallow bowl and beat lightly.

2 In a large, nonstick frying pan over medium-high heat, melt the 2 teaspoons butter in the olive oil.

3 While the oil and butter are heating (don't let the butter burn), dip the fish in the flour, turning to coat both sides and shaking off any excess, then dip each fillet in the egg, letting the excess egg drip back into the bowl. Place the fish in the hot pan and reduce the heat to medium-low.

4   Cook until the bottom of the fillets are nicely browned, about 4 minutes. Using a wide spatula, turn the fillets carefully and continue cooking until opaque throughout, 3 to 4 minutes longer.

5   Transfer the fish to 2 plates and keep warm. Wipe out the frying pan with a paper towel and place over low heat. Add the 3 tablespoons butter, the capers, the parsley, and the lemon juice to the pan. Swirl the pan over the heat until the butter melts. Drizzle the butter sauce over the fish and serve right away, with the lemon wedges.

ROAST CHICKEN WITH ARUGULA AND BREAD SALAD

Restaurants come and go with dazzling speed in San Francisco, as trends and tastes shift and change. Yet walk into Zuni Café, which opened on Market Street in 1979, and whether it's your first visit or your fiftieth, you'll instantly feel like you're in the right place. The atmosphere is effervescent, the conversation lively. And out of the kitchen comes a steady stream of the famous Zuni roast chicken, each bronzed bird nestled into a chunky salad of levain bread, currants, and arugula. Even without a wood-burning oven like Zuni's, the technique developed by the late Judy Rodgers, Zuni's head chef and co-owner, produces a remarkable bird with a true taste of the good life. This recipe is a simplified version inspired by Rodgers's original.

SERVES 3 OR 4

1 chicken, about 3 pounds, preferable organic and/or pasture-raised

4 sprigs fresh rosemary, sage, or thyme

Kosher salt and freshly ground black pepper

FOR THE BREAD SALAD:

½ loaf (about ½ pound) day-old levain or sourdough bread, crusts removed

½ cup olive oil, plus 1 tablespoon

4 scallions, white and tender green parts only, thinly sliced

2 cloves garlic, thinly sliced

¼ cup homemade or low-sodium chicken stock

1½ tablespoons red wine vinegar

Kosher salt and freshly ground black pepper

5 cups baby kale or other sturdy baby greens

1 | Season the chicken: Loosen the skin of the breasts and thighs by wiggling a finger under the skin. Tuck an herb sprig under the skin of each breast and thigh. Season the chicken well with salt and pepper. For best results, cover loosely and refrigerate for 1 to 2 days before cooking.

2 When you're ready to cook, preheat the broiler. To make the bread salad, divide the bread into 4 large pieces and brush with ¼ cup of the olive oil. Place on a baking sheet and broil until lightly toasted and golden, about 2 minutes. Tear into bite-sized pieces; you should have about 4 cups. Place in a large bowl. Reduce the oven temperature to 475°F.

3 In a small frying pan over low heat, heat the 1 tablespoon olive oil. Add the scallions and garlic and cook, stirring, until softened but not browned. Add the scallion mixture and chicken stock to the bowl with the bread chunks and toss to mix well.

4 In a small bowl, whisk together the remaining ¼ cup olive oil and the vinegar. Season with salt and pepper. Add 2 tablespoons of the vinaigrette to the bread mixture and toss well. Place the bread in a baking dish, cover loosely with aluminum foil, and set aside.

5 Heat a 10-inch cast-iron skillet in the oven until very hot, about 10 minutes. Pat the chicken dry and carefully place in the skillet, breast-side up.

6 Roast for 30 minutes, then flip the chicken over, breast-side down; cook for 10 to 15 minutes. Flip the chicken, breast-side up, and cook until the skin is crisped and well browned, 5 to 10 minutes longer. The total roasting time will be 45 to 55 minutes. Transfer the chicken to a platter and set aside. Let any juices drain from the cavity of the chicken into the skillet.

7 Reduce the oven temperature to 300°F. Place the bread salad in the oven. Bake until warmed through, about 10 minutes.

8 Pour off the excess fat from the chicken skillet, leaving the sticky brown drippings. Place the skillet over medium heat and heat, stirring to loosen the drippings, for 1 to 2 minutes.

9 Transfer the bread salad to a bowl, add the chicken pan drippings, the kale, and the remaining vinaigrette. Toss well. Arrange the bread salad around the chicken and serve right away.

JOE'S SPECIAL

This is an old-school dish, the sort of thing thrown together by generations of California cooks for a simple but satisfying weekday supper or hearty weekend breakfast. It was a specialty of the house at New Joe's, a San Francisco restaurant popular in the 1920s, and its successor, Original Joe's. We've updated it a little by using fresh chard instead of the usual frozen spinach, but frozen spinach is certainly great in a pinch. If you're using frozen spinach, thaw and squeeze it very dry before using.

SERVES 2–4

2 tablespoons olive oil

1 yellow onion, finely chopped

3 cloves garlic, minced

8 ounces ground beef or turkey

3 bunches chard, tough stems removed, leaves torn into bite-sized pieces

8 large eggs, beaten

Kosher salt and freshly ground black pepper

¼ cup freshly grated Parmesan cheese

1 In a large skillet, heat the olive oil over medium-high heat. Add the onion and cook, stirring, until soft and translucent, about 5 minutes. Add the garlic and ground beef and cook, stirring, until any liquid is evaporated and meat is browned, 6 to 9 minutes.

2 Add the chard and cook, stirring until gently wilted. Add the eggs and cook, stirring often, until the eggs are cooked through and mixture is no longer wet, about 5 minutes. Season with salt and pepper. Sprinkle with the Parmesan and serve right away.

RICE PILAF WITH TOASTED NOODLES

In the 1940s, Tom and Lois DeDomenico were newlyweds in San Francisco. Tom worked at the Golden Grain Macaroni Company, his family's pasta business. Left alone at home, his young, pregnant wife Lois started to watch and learn to cook from their Armenian landlady, Pailadzo Captanian, who had fled from the genocide in Turkey in 1915.

Mrs. Captanian cooked the foods she knew: stuffed grape leaves, homemade yogurt, braised lamb, and a rice-and-noodle dish she called *pilaf*. Tom DeDomenico would come home with extra pasta from the factory, and Mrs. Captanian would break up the dry noodles, brown them deeply in butter with a handful of rice, then add chicken stock and cook until tender. This pilaf became the DeDomenicos favorite dish, and before long, Tom took the idea to the factory's test kitchens. By the 1950s, Rice-A-Roni was in supermarkets across the country, and an Armenian woman's taste of home was America's favorite new convenience food.

SERVES 6

6 tablespoons unsalted butter

4 ounces angel hair pasta, broken into small pieces

2 cups long-grain rice

3½ cups chicken stock

Kosher salt and freshly ground black pepper

¼ cup chopped fresh flat-leaf parsley

1 In a large saucepan over medium heat, melt the butter. Add the pasta and cook, stirring, until the pasta is deep brown and very crunchy, about 5 to 6 minutes.

2 Add the rice and stir to coat with butter. Add the stock, stir, and bring to a simmer. Cover the pan with a tight-fitting lid. Reduce the heat to low. Cook until the rice is tender and the liquid is absorbed, about 12 minutes.

3 Remove from the heat and let cool slightly. Toss gently to fluff the grains, season with salt and pepper to taste, and stir in the parsley. Serve right away.

CIOPPINO

Many people consider *cioppino* (pronounced "chu-PEE-no") to be the ultimate San Francisco dish. Served in wharfside restaurants, it arrives in a jumbo-sized bowl overflowing with mussels, clams, shrimp, fish, and big chunks of Dungeness crab in the shell, bathed in a garlic-tomato sauce. The original *cioppino*, though, was a straightforward fishermen's dish. Back when Fishermen's Wharf really was a working wharf, the crews were mostly Italians from Genoa along the Mediterranean coast. Out on the rough Pacific for days at a time, these hard-working sailors prided themselves on their interpretation of a Genovese fish soup, *ciuppin*. Onions, garlic, tomato paste, a bit of oregano, and fish fresh from the sea were cooked fast and hot into a meal fit for a hungry man, with a final drizzle of olive oil to add the civilizing Italian touch.

SERVES 4

¼ cup olive oil, plus more for drizzling

1 yellow onion, thinly sliced

1 head fennel, cored and thinly sliced

2 cloves garlic, thinly sliced

1 teaspoon red pepper flakes

1 teaspoon dried oregano

1 cup dry, full-bodied red wine such as Zinfandel

One 28-ounce can diced plum tomatoes, with juice

2 tablespoons chopped fresh flat-leaf parsley

1 teaspoon kosher salt

1 pound firm, meaty fish such as lingcod, rockfish, or halibut, cut into bite-sized pieces

1 pound mussels, scrubbed and debearded, or 1 pound small clams, scrubbed and rinsed

1 to 1½ pounds Dungeness crab, cooked, cleaned, and cracked

Crusty sourdough bread for serving

continued

1 In a heavy-bottomed saucepan or Dutch oven, heat the olive oil over medium heat. Add the onion and fennel and cook, stirring, until the onion is softened and beginning to brown, about 8 minutes. Add the garlic, red pepper flakes, and oregano and cook until fragrant, about 2 minutes longer.

2 Raise the heat to medium-high. Add the wine, bring to a simmer, and cook until slightly reduced, about 8 minutes. Add the tomatoes and their juices, the parsley, and the salt; return to a simmer and cook until slightly reduced and flavorful, about 10 minutes.

3 Add the fish and mussels and cook until the fish is opaque throughout and the mussels have opened, 5 to 8 minutes. (Discard any mussels that do not open.) Add the crab and cook for another minute or so until heated through.

4 Divide the *cioppino* among 4 large, shallow soup bowls. Drizzle with olive oil and serve right away with the bread.

WHOLE STEAMED FISH WITH GINGER AND GARLIC

Since the 1860s, San Francisco's Chinese community has celebrated the Lunar New Year with an elaborate parade full of brilliantly colored floats, firecrackers, lion dancers, and a 268-foot-long golden dragon carried by over 100 people. Families come together to share good-luck rituals for the coming year; this head-on fish is a symbol of abundance and prosperity.

SERVES 4

One 2- to 2½-pound whole head-on fish such as sea bass, rockfish, or snapper, cleaned

5 scallions, white parts only, very thinly sliced

One 2-inch piece fresh ginger, peeled and grated

2 cloves garlic, minced

3 tablespoons light soy sauce

2 tablespoons Chinese rice wine or sherry

1 tablespoon vegetable oil

Fresh cilantro sprigs for garnish

1 Place the fish on a cutting board. Using a sharp knife, cut deep slashes on the diagonal across both sides, spacing them about 1 inch apart. Place the fish on a large, heatproof plate that will fit inside your steamer or wok. Place about half of the scallions and one-third of the ginger and garlic inside the cavity of the fish. Spread half of the remaining scallions and all of the remaining ginger and garlic over the top. Pour the soy sauce, rice wine, and oil evenly over the fish.

2 Bring about 2 inches of water to a boil in the base of a steamer or wok. Set the plate in the steamer, cover tightly, reduce the heat so the water continues to simmer, and steam for 15 to 18 minutes. To test for doneness, insert the tip of a knife into the thickest part of the fish below the head. If it penetrates easily and no pink shows, the fish is done.

3 Using oven mitts to protect your hands, carefully remove the plate from the steamer. Divide the fish among 4 plates, garnish with the remaining scallions and the cilantro, and serve right away.

SWEETS

Don't let all those kale salads fool you; San Francisco has a sweet tooth that just won't quit. Even on most shivery, fog-wrapped days, people clamber for ice-cream cones in flavors from green tea and black sesame to lavender honey and balsamic strawberry. Teens flirt and text over candy-colored drinks in bright bubble-tea shops, while the Italian cafes and bakeries of North Beach pair frothy cappuccinos with crunchy biscotti and creamy tiramisù.

There are sweets to suit every taste and culture, from pastel-hued Japanese mochi to piping-hot egg custard tarts and moon cakes filled with red bean or lotus seed paste. Shell-shaped conchas and other pan dulce are heaped in the windows of the panaderias along 24th Street in the Mission while pushcart vendors offer the cooling, sweet-and-spicy popsicles known as paletas. Out in the Richmond, Russian and Polish bakeries serve up cheesecake, poppyseed strudel, and caraway-studded rye bread.

Long the home of Guittard and Ghirardelli, the Bay Area now hosts several notable bean-to-bar artisanal chocolate makers. And for home bakers and pastry chefs alike, the city's many farmers' markets are a paradise of inspiration, thanks to a year-round growing season that lights up even the drabbest winter day with tangy kumquats and fragrant Meyer lemons.

51

MEYER LEMON RICOTTA PANCAKES

Light, moist, and extra-lemony, these delicate ricotta pancakes are a must-have morning dish and an extraordinarily popular brunch pick. But they also make an excellent dessert when topped with lemon curd and a dusting of powdered sugar. Since wild blackberries grow all over the city from Bernal Hill to China Beach, it's nice to add a handful to the pancake batter.

Meyer lemons are deeply fragrant and sweeter than the more common Eureka variety; if you don't have a Meyer lemon tree in your backyard, you can use a supermarket lemon instead, but halve the amount of zest and juice.

MAKES ABOUT 12 PANCAKES; SERVES 4

1 cup ricotta cheese

¼ cup milk

3 large eggs, separated

2 tablespoons sugar

⅛ teaspoon kosher salt

1 tablespoon finely grated Meyer lemon zest

1 tablespoon fresh Meyer lemon juice

1 teaspoon vanilla extract

½ cup plus 1 tablespoon all-purpose flour

2 tablespoons unsalted butter, melted

1 cup blackberries

1 In a large bowl, whisk together the ricotta, milk, egg yolks, sugar, salt, lemon zest and juice, and vanilla. Stir in the flour and melted butter until just combined.

2 In a separate bowl, using a whisk or hand-held electric mixer, beat the egg whites until they hold soft peaks. Using a rubber spatula, fold the egg whites into the ricotta mixture.

3 Lightly grease a griddle or wide skillet and heat over medium-low heat. Using a quarter-cup measure, spoon out circles of batter. Add a few blackberries to each pancake. Cook until the bottoms are golden brown, about 2 minutes. Flip and continue cooking for another 2 minutes, until both sides are golden. Repeat to use the remaining batter. Serve warm.

AFFOGATO

Brilliantly easy, magically delicious: this two-ingredient Italian invention is served in San Francisco cafés from North Beach and beyond. Taking its name from the Italian word for "drowned," an *affogato* is a scoop of gelato—typically vanilla, but pick your favorite—drowned in a freshly made shot of hot espresso. The bitter coffee melts just enough of the sweet gelato to make a creamy moat around the scoop.

SERVES 1

1 scoop vanilla gelato or ice cream, or your favorite flavor

1 shot hot freshly brewed espresso

1 Place the gelato or ice cream in a small, deep bowl. Pour the shot of espresso over the gelato and serve right away.

BALSAMIC STRAWBERRY ICE CREAM

Ruby-red strawberries, as fragrant as they are sweet, are a delicious part of San Francisco's farmers' markets from spring to early fall. Shoppers can choose between many varieties with enticing names like Albion, Camorosa, Chandler, Tri-Star, or Seascape. This ice cream, inspired by a recipe from Bi-Rite Creamery in the Mission, uses an Italian trick to boost the berries' flavor: a splash of balsamic vinegar.

MAKES ABOUT 1 QUART; SERVES 6 TO 8

2 pints ripe strawberries, hulled and quartered (about 3 cups)

3 tablespoons sugar, plus ½ cup

3 teaspoons balsamic vinegar

5 large egg yolks

1½ cups heavy cream

1 cup whole milk

¼ teaspoon kosher salt

1 In a bowl, combine the berries, the 3 tablespoons sugar, and 2 teaspoons of the vinegar. Let stand until the berries start to release their juices, about 15 minutes.

2 Transfer the berries and their liquid to a saucepan, place over medium heat, and cook, stirring often, until the mixture is jammy, 5 to 7 minutes. Remove from the heat and let cool. Pour the mixture into a blender and process briefly to form a coarse purée. Cover and chill.

3 To make the custard, in a heatproof bowl, whisk together the egg yolks and ¼ cup of the sugar. Set aside. In a heavy saucepan over medium heat, combine the cream, milk, salt, and remaining ¼ cup sugar and heat until just steaming, stirring to dissolve the sugar.

4 Ladle out about 1 cup of the hot cream mixture and, pouring slowly, whisk it into the egg mixture. Pour the egg and cream mixture back into the saucepan and cook, stirring constantly, until the mixture is thick enough to coat the back of a spoon, 1 to 2 minutes. Remove from the heat and pour the custard through a fine-mesh sieve. Let cool, then refrigerate until well chilled, at least 2 hours or up to overnight.

5 Whisk the strawberry purée and the remaining 1 teaspoon vinegar into the chilled custard. Freeze the mixture in an ice-cream machine according to the manufacturer's instructions. Serve right away for a softer ice cream, or transfer to an airtight container and freeze until firm, about 2 hours, or for up to 3 weeks.

MORNING BUNS

A cup of steaming coffee or tea, a fragrant, flaky morning bun: that's our favorite way to start a day by the Bay. These days, any San Francisco foodie's bucket list has to include the delectable buns from can't-miss destinations like La Farine, Tartine, and Arsicault Bakery.

To ensure maximum flakiness, start the dough the day before you want to serve the buns. Let the dough chill overnight before filling and baking.

MAKES 10 BUNS

FOR THE DOUGH:

2¼ teaspoons (1 packet) active dry yeast

2 tablespoons lukewarm water

1 large egg, beaten

¼ cup whole milk

1½ cups all-purpose flour, plus more for dusting

2 tablespoons granulated sugar

1 teaspoon kosher salt

14 tablespoons (1¾ sticks) cold unsalted butter, cut into cubes

FOR ASSEMBLY:

Room-temperature butter or nonstick cooking spray for greasing

½ cup granulated sugar, plus ⅓ cup

¼ cup packed brown sugar

2 teaspoons ground cinnamon

Grated zest of 1 orange

1   To make the dough, in a small bowl, sprinkle the yeast over the warm water and let stand until the yeast is a little foamy, about 5 minutes. Whisk to dissolve, then whisk in the egg and milk. Set aside.

2   In a large bowl, whisk together the flour, granulated sugar, and salt. Add the butter pieces and toss to coat in the flour mixture. Using a pastry blender or your fingers, cut or pinch in the butter until more or less uniformly combined and the mixture is clumped into bits about the size of peas.

3 Drizzle the yeast mixture over the flour mixture and stir just until a shaggy dough comes together; it will be moist and soft. Cover the bowl tightly with plastic wrap and refrigerate for 2 hours.

4 Dust a work surface with flour. Remove the dough from the refrigerator and turn out onto the work surface. Dust the dough and a rolling pin with flour and roll the dough out into a rectangle about 9 by 12 inches, with the short side facing you. The dough will be rough at first, but will smooth out as you roll. As if you were folding a letter, fold the top third down towards the middle, then fold the bottom third up. Turn the dough 90 degrees. Roll out to its original size. Continue folding, turning, and rolling. If the dough becomes too springy to roll, wrap it up again and return to the refrigerator for about an hour to relax. Repeat the rolling, folding, and turning of the dough for a total of 6 times. Wrap the finished dough rectangle in plastic wrap and refrigerate for at least 2 hours or up to overnight.

5 To assemble the buns, grease a standard 12-cup muffin pan with butter. In a small bowl, whisk together the ½ cup granulated sugar, the brown sugar, 1½ teaspoons of the cinnamon, and the orange zest and set aside.

6 Dust a clean work surface with flour. Unwrap the dough and place on the work surface. Roll out into a slightly larger rectangle, about 12 by 16 inches, with the long end facing you this time. Sprinkle the brown sugar mixture evenly across the dough. Starting at the long end, roll the dough away from you into a tight cylinder. Wet the seams and press the edges together to keep the log from unrolling. Using a serrated knife, cut the log crosswise into 10 to 12 rounds, each 1½ to 1¾ inches thick. Tuck the rounds into the prepared muffin cups. Let rise in a warm place until puffy and doubled in size, about 2 hours.

7 Preheat oven to 350°F. In a shallow bowl, whisk together the ⅓ cup granulated sugar and the remaining ½ teaspoon cinnamon and set aside.

8 Bake the buns until deep golden brown, about 20 minutes. Transfer to a wire rack and let cool slightly, then remove the buns from pan while still hot and roll in the cinnamon sugar to coat.

TIRAMISÙ

Tiramisù means "pick me up" in Italian, a reference to the strong espresso that ripples through this layered dessert of ladyfingers, custard, and rich, sweet marscapone cheese. Because it holds up well, and gets even better after a day in the fridge, it's a sweet treat that can be found on the menu of every North Beach café, perfect for pairing with a freshly pulled espresso.

Mascarpone is a fresh Italian cream cheese with a flavor somewhere between butter and cream; you can find good-quality domestic brands in specialty grocery stores and well-stocked supermarkets.

SERVES 6

FOR THE CUSTARD:

1 large egg plus 3 large egg yolks

¼ cup white wine, preferably a sweet one like Moscato or Moscato d'asti

¼ cup dry Marsala wine

2 tablespoons amaretto or dark rum

⅓ cup sugar

1 tablespoon brewed espresso or very strong coffee

1 teaspoon vanilla extract

1 cup mascarpone cheese, at room temperature

FOR THE SYRUP:

¾ cup brewed espresso or very strong coffee

1½ tablespoons sugar

1 tablespoon unsweetened cocoa powder, such as Ghirardelli or Guittard

1 tablespoons dark rum (optional)

30 Italian-style ladyfingers *(savoiardi)*

¼ cup unsweetened cocoa powder

1 To make the custard, in a double boiler over medium-low heat, whisk together the egg, egg yolks, sweet white wine, Marsala, and amaretto. Keep whisking until the mixture foams up and thickens enough to stand up in a spoon. Remove the top of the double boiler from the heat. Continue whisking for 2 minutes.

continued

2 Whisk in the sugar, espresso, and vanilla. Fold in the mascarpone, about ¼ cup at a time, until thoroughly blended. Set aside.

3 To make the syrup, in a wide, shallow bowl, combine the espresso, sugar, cocoa powder, and rum, if using. Immerse the ladyfingers in the syrup to moisten fully.

4 To assemble the tiramisù, cover the bottom of an 8-inch-square baking dish with a layer of the soaked ladyfingers. Spoon half the custard mixture over the ladyfingers. Top with another layer of soaked ladyfingers, laid perpendicular to the first layer. Add the remaining custard. Sift a generous layer of cocoa powder over the top. Cover and refrigerate until set and well chilled, at least 4 hours and up to 12, before serving.

HONG KONG-STYLE EGG TARTS

Also known as *dan tats* or *dan tas*, these delicate, flaky custard tarts make
a perfect sweet finish to a dim sum lunch. At the popular Golden Gate
Bakery, the line often stretches down Grant Avenue as hopefuls wait for
their turn to fill a bright-pink bakery box with fresh-from-the-oven *dan tas*.
While most Chinatown bakeries use a two-stage dough (typically called
"oil dough" and "water dough") to create a tart crust that's both flaky and
tender, we've found that high-quality frozen puff pastry gives a very similar
result. These tarts are best when they're just about one or two bites each,
so use fluted tartlet (mini) pans, about 2 to 3 inches in diameter.

MAKES 12 SMALL TARTS; SERVES 6

1 sheet puff pastry,
thawed if frozen

½ cup sugar

4 large eggs

¼ cup evaporated milk

½ teaspoon vanilla extract

Kosher salt

1 Preheat the oven to 350°F. Have ready 12 mini tartlet pans, 2 to 3 inches in
diameter. Roll out the puff pastry into a sheet about ¼ inch thick. Cut the
pastry into rounds just slightly larger than your tart pans. Gently press the
pastry rounds into the pans. Arrange the tart shells on a baking sheet and
place in the refrigerator while you make the filling.

2 In a saucepan, combine the sugar and 1 cup water over medium heat and
cook, stirring occasionally, until the sugar dissolves and mixture is clear,
3 to 5 minutes. Pour into a large heatproof bowl. Set aside and let cool.

3 Whisk the eggs into cooled sugar syrup, then whisk in the evaporated
milk, vanilla, and a pinch of salt. Strain through a fine-mesh strainer into
a pitcher or large measuring cup.

4 Fill each chilled tart shell three-fourths full with the custard mixture. Bake
until crust is puffed and pale gold and filling is set but still slightly jiggly,
35 to 40 minutes. Transfer to a wire rack and let cool for 10 minutes, then
gently remove the tartlets from the pans and serve.

OATMEAL COOKIE ICE CREAM SANDWICHES

Anyone lucky enough to grow up in San Francisco knows about It's-It. These chocolate-coated ice cream sandwiches have been a San Francisco staple since 1928, invented by a vendor at Playland-at-the-Beach, a popular amusement park along Ocean Beach. Crunchy oatmeal cookies sandwich a choice of seven ice cream flavors, including green tea and cappuccino, that reflect the city's diverse tastes. While the company now distributes and ships far beyond the Bay Area, it's fun to try out a homemade version by pairing your favorite ice cream with thin, crispy oatmeal cookies and a dunk in melted chocolate.

MAKES 12 ICE-CREAM SANDWICHES

1 cup all-purpose flour or whole-wheat pastry flour

½ teaspoon baking powder

½ teaspoon baking soda

½ teaspoon kosher salt

¼ teaspoon ground cinnamon

12 tablespoons (1½ sticks) unsalted butter, at room temperature

¾ cup granulated sugar

¼ cup packed brown sugar

1 large egg

1 teaspoon vanilla extract

2 cups old-fashioned rolled oats

1½ pints ice cream of your choice (see recipe introduction), softened

12 ounces dark chocolate, chopped

2 tablespoons coconut oil or canola oil

1 Preheat the oven to 350°F. In a bowl, whisk together the flour, baking powder, baking soda, salt, and cinnamon. Set aside.

2 In a bowl, using a stand mixer or hand-held electric mixer, cream together the butter, granulated sugar, and brown sugar until fluffy. Beat in the egg and vanilla. Add the flour mixture and beat on low speed until just combined. Add the oats and beat until just combined.

4 Scoop the batter into even balls (about 1½ tablespoons per cookie) and arrange on a baking sheet, leaving about 2 inches of space between them. Flatten gently with your palm. Bake until the cookies are golden brown at the edges, 12 to 15 minutes. Transfer to a wire rack and let cool slightly on the pan, then transfer the cookies to the rack and let cool completely.

5 Place the cookies in the freezer until very cold, about 30 minutes. Spread a layer of the softened ice cream on the bottom of a cookie about 1 inch thick, then top with another cookie. Repeat with the remaining cookies. Return the cookies to the freezer for several hours, or until very firm.

6 Line a baking sheet that will fit in the freezer with parchment or wax paper. In a double boiler or microwave, melt the chocolate with the oil over medium heat, stirring occasionally to help the chocolate melt. Remove the chocolate mixture from the heat and let cool to room temperature. Dunk each ice cream sandwich into the chocolate to coat, then place on the prepared baking sheet. Repeat with the remaining sandwiches. Freeze until the chocolate is firm, about 1 hour.

PALETAS

Scorching days may be a rarity in San Francisco, but so is air-conditioning. On those rare hot days that stay hot even through the evening, nothing beats the heat like a *paleta*, refreshing Mexican-style popsicles. Bought from corner grocery stores in the Mission or roaming hand-pushed carts in Dolores Park and other corners, these not-too-sweet treats come in dozens of enticing flavors, such as sweet-tart tamarind, spicy cucumber-chile, creamy coconut, and tropical mango.

EACH RECIPE MAKES 8 *PALETAS*

MANGO

1 cup mango nectar

3 tablespoons sugar

1 tablespoon fresh lemon or lime juice

1 fresh mango, peeled, seeded, and diced

1 In a small saucepan over medium heat, combine the mango nectar, sugar, lemon juice, and ½ cup water. Cook, stirring occasionally, until the sugar is dissolved, about 5 minutes. Remove from the heat and let cool, then refrigerate until well chilled, about 2 hours.

2 Stir the fresh mango into the chilled juice mixture. Divide the mixture evenly among 8 popsicle molds. Insert popsicle sticks or handles and freeze until firm, about 4 hours and up to 3 days.

CUCUMBER-CHILE

3 large cucumbers (about 3 pounds total) peeled, seeded, and chopped

¼ cup fresh lime juice

1 tablespoon sugar

1 teaspoon chile powder

½ teaspoon kosher salt

1 Measure out ½ cup of the chopped cucumber and set aside. In a blender, process the remaining cucumber until smooth. Strain the puréed cucumber through a fine-mesh sieve placed over a bowl. You should have about 2 cups juice.

2 Add the lime juice, sugar, chile powder, salt, and reserved cucumber pieces to the bowl with the cucumber juice. Stir until the sugar is dissolved.

3 Divide the mixture evenly among 8 popsicle molds. Insert popsicle sticks or handles and freeze until firm, about 4 hours and up to 3 days.

INDEX